Look At What's Inside

Mark Jamnik

DEDICATION

This book is dedicated for those willing to be curious and do the courageous deep work, inside. It's inviting you to question and challenge who you think you are, to discover who you really are...the creative inside. This is for those who choose to sit in that uncomfortable silence to hear the quite still inner voice. That voice that lets you know you are on the right track and/ or the discernment to recognize you have been listening to a much louder voice, outside of you...the voice of what society has sold you over the years. This is an invitation for you to look at what's inside and uncover what has been covered up through the outer successes, and begin see the things that makes your soul sing. To do this inner work, it takes energy, effort, investment and in many cases years, even decades with sometimes "seemingly" little results outside. I honor your quest to look at what's inside.

CONTENTS

ACKNOWLEDGMENTS

This is to family, friends and acquaintances I have met along the way where we invest the time and distance to stay in touch. This is to those that I have celebrated with and also cried with when my dream to help people seemed difficult. You know who you are. I LOVE YOU! I love reading books and something I have observed about the acknowledgment section of any book is there are always heartfelt names and messages to those closest to them.

1. CALLING YOUR INNER ARTIST

Purpose

"It is a beautiful truth that all men contain something of the artist in them." Walt Witman.

Yes, we are all artists.

Even if you don't think you are an artist … an artist resides in each of us.

This book is a calling to your inner artist.

I invite you to read along and hear and feel the longing from within.

It's up to you to heed the call, or continue to ignore it.

I hope you choose to heed it. After all, I wrote this for a part of you that you might not have accessed in a while. You might not even think it's there and yet, you picked up this book. Well done!

You are reading from a deeper part of you.

The artist inside has been wanting you to connect with them for a long time.

The artist I'm referring to for you MAY be different than my artist who loves to paint.

Years ago, I heeded that inner calling of something I didn't know was calling. Before hearing the call, I had never painted before.

The first time I painted, the best way I can share it was what I said out loud: "I feel like I started breathing again." While that comment may sound a bit extreme, it's difficult to describe the feeling I experienced, so those words most closely express what I felt.

In that moment ... gone were all of the tasks and everything happening in my life; it was me and the canvas.

The present moment is so beautiful and available in abundance to ALL of us.

The invitation for you throughout this book is to connect to your inner artist, whatever that inner artist is; maybe you'll pick up a paint brush, or begin drawing again, or write that novel you want to write, or take your camera and snap some pictures, or dust off that old musical instrument ... whatever is art to you ... that is who I invite you to stop "starving" them and start feeding that creative side. ALL for the sake of creating, for the joy of creating.

This is a call to create something outside of yourself that has been waiting to be expressed from the inside.

Consumerism versus creation

Disclaimer: I'm going to make some "gross generalizations and assumptions" as I express how "most" people – and this does not mean everyone – do not fit in the same box.

Disclaimer 2: I'm NOT making owning things wrong. A friend, Jon, shared with me in 2020: "It's ok to have things, just don't let things have you."

Now that this is out of the way, let's continue.

Today's world has been so driven towards consumerism that creativity is something most rely on others to provide.

Consumerism is what causes many to buy items such as branded clothing to more luxury items such as cars or custom homes. After all, these kinds of purchases are so well marketed and that feeling of buying has become addictive; HIGHLY addictive.

By buying, you may feel like you are feeding something, yet ... it is teaching you joy and fulfillment come from outside. When you feed your inner artist that is starving, you discover a joy and fulfillment that can only come from within.

The quote: *"We are taught to be consumers ... creators are who we are"* flowed from me one morning as I was in the process of writing this book.

Someone else creates a beautiful item and you want to own it because you love the look of it or the story of it. Instead of it being an item, the story brings it to life.

Art reflects life.

As an example, I own a pair of Persol sunglasses; they are nice sunglasses, not inexpensive sunglasses and not super expensive either, which I know is all relative. I think I paid $180 for them and have owned them for 6 years, as of this writing.

Why did I buy them? Sure, I liked the way they looked and I needed new sunglasses; my previous Oakley's that I owned for over 8 years needed to be replaced. The reason why I really bought the Persols, though, was because of the story I heard of how they are built. When I was shopping and looking at the different sunglasses, I was informed by the salesperson the Persols are all hand assembled and because of that, each pair takes 8 days to build from start to finish. I reviewed the website and loved hearing the story!

They aren't sunglasses to me, they are an expression of someone's artistry. There is an artistry in the making of each pair and someone invested part of their life in hand crafting them.

Think about that: someone hand crafted sunglasses I wear each day; they are an extension of someone's love of the craft of creating sunglasses.

They are less sunglasses and more of an artistic expression of someone's passion in creating beauty.

"Inner" Reflection Exercises

Take a moment and think of a recent item that meant something to you. Write your answer in the blanks:

What was it? _____

What caused YOU to choose it? _____

How is it reflecting something deep down that you are looking to express? _____

The goal behind this book is to look inside to see that inner artist to create a masterpiece ...

A masterpiece of YOUR life.

By the end of this book, you'll see how looking at the seeming "messes" in your life create the masterpiece of your life.

Decide and allow yourself to see art being expressed differently through your life, whether that is "hand crafting sunglasses" as a profession, or painting for fun or anything in between that allows you to express your inner artist.

This book is about the artist that creates the art.

To begin, let's take a look at what we think of artists.

2. THE "STARVING ARTIST"

When most think of artists, the phrase many people closely link is ... "starving."

The "starving artist."

Isn't it interesting that "starving artist" are the two most commonly combined words when you think of an artist?

That causes many to RUN as far away from art as possible.

For years, it's what I did.

No one wants to "starve."

Starving doesn't sound pleasant, so many run from it.

You can only run for so long before you get tired.

Maybe you have been running from it for too long and it's what caused you to pick up this book.

It's why you are still reading it (great job, by the way).

There may be an unquenchable hunger inside and you can't quite put your finger on what the hunger is.

Because you have read to this point, I invite you to see that "starving artist" phrase differently ... in a way you haven't seen it before.

What you have "been taught" and what "you bought"
What if hearing and "buying" the term of a "starving artist" that "society" has taught you that you bought caused you to run and "starve" the creativity inside your own inner "artist"?

If you are not expressing your creativity … you are a "starving artist" … and the starving isn't at all what you thought it was.

Introducing the "starving 'inner' artist."

You bought … and bought … and bought … what you have been taught throughout your life.

In the process, you were starving your creativity and feeding it consumption instead.

You have been taught to consume and consumption constantly needs to be fed.

Hmmm … something to think about.

What my "starving inner artist" looked like.
It was 2015, and I was living in a beautiful high-rise condo for the past 7 years. It was a beautiful glass beacon of elegance and simplicity (in my eyes) by the lake (in the Arizona desert) close to downtown Tempe. I could see Sun Devil stadium (home of the Arizona State University football team) from my home.

I was standing by the glass door to my balcony while talking on the phone with a good friend, Matt, and I said, "I see people walking the banks of Tempe Town Lake by my place all day long. I see them looking at the building, pointing, saying, 'wouldn't it be cool to live there?' Or 'wouldn't it be cool to live there?' I am projecting those statements because it's what I said when I saw the first building go up on the lake. Before I owned … I said, 'Wow, I would LOVE to live there.'"

Shortly after, I paused, looking out at the water, and said, "Matt, I feel like I'm in prison.

"I know I can go outside, walk around. There is a lot of activity going on around me, yet for some reason, I feel like I'm in prison."

The language might sound odd – it was to me at the time as well – though those words came up and I wanted to take time to process and observe them so I could dig deeper and see what inside was causing me to say those words.

I didn't realize why I was in prison; I began looking inside and would later find out why in 2020 … more on that in a little bit.

I was so constricted. I made the constriction.

I bought everything that the world said would make me happy and for some reason, I felt stuck.

I needed to work and work and work to pay for my place. I had everything in its perfect place. When friends came over, they would say it looked like a model home. It looked PERFECT on the outside, yet I wasn't sharing the INSIDE of prison when they commented on how beautiful everything looked.

The biggest question I was focused on for years was, "How do I keep this outer world looking perfect for others to see?"

It looked beautiful. I was covering up the inner "mess" underneath; the feelings of "how am I going to keep paying for this …"

Here is a picture I took in early 2021 of the "glamor shot" of what my prison looked like.

I was taking pictures to sell my car and I also wanted to capture the picture of my car, home, wardrobe; everything that I wanted to portray to the outer world.

- 2013 Audi S4, 6 speed manual with perfect paint (you could drive it into a showroom)

- High rise condo by the lake

- Banana Republic labeled clothes

As an aside, once I snapped this picture, I KNEW I was going to use it somehow, some way in the future, not knowing it would end up in a book.

Ok ... and we're back.

Building (slow) momentum ...

Now, I had started painting in 2011 and I was beginning to feed my inner artist, but once a year wasn't fueling my soul.

I am sharing my story that was happening deep down and only after something that art expressed through me opened me in a way for me to break free.

Many people these days have a "starving inner artist" and attempt to feed it with consumable goods, creating a silent prison of their own making.

Let me clarify and repeat something that I mentioned earlier ...

I am NOT making nice things wrong, or having nice things wrong. I LOVE nice things. I HAVE nice things, I told you the story of my

Persol sunglasses. I have goals to own other nice things; I LOVE the look of a Porsche 911. I would love to own a 991 or 992 model with a 7 speed manual … YES, a manual … I love driving manual transmissions using every appendage. AND if the value I create in the world affords me the ability to do it, great, If not … that's fine I have an inner love that the 911 will never fuel.

In 2022, I bought a very expensive mountain bike because I love spending time outside and VERY regularly use it. I own nice furniture, I buy high quality clothing that lasts for a long time. For instance, I still have a North Face T-shirt that I bought in 2008 … and wear it while mountain biking.

To repeat, I am not making it wrong to have nice things … "it's okay to have things, just don't let things have you."

I heard that in 2019 and in early 2020.

With a wink …"do you remember what happened in 2020?"

Not a quarantine, this is a chrysalis

Yes, I was stuck at home. We were all stuck at home.

I made a VERY CONSCIOUS decision before locking myself inside at the onset of the experience. I had been doing personal development for over 10 years to this point so I had been working on my mindset.

I shared with many I spoke to online, "This is not a quarantine, this is a chrysalis."

That was the mindset I made before I locked myself inside for a couple weeks.

While I was stuck in my home … something very interesting happened.

Remember that story from 2015, where I shared my home was a prison … the same home became my freedom.

During that time from 2015 to 2020, I was painting approximately 1 work a year. 1 A YEAR!

During the time home in 2020, I fed my starving inner artist and I bought a bunch of canvases and that year I painted, and painted and painted ... and painted some more.

I painted 26 works in 2020! 26 in a Year!

My inner artist began healing ... the paintings I did in 2020 opened me up to something deep down that I NEVER EXPECTED! And it happened in December of that year.

In December, I didn't travel to visit my family like I had for the 17 years prior. Instead, I said, "I'm going to do a staycation" and have my first Christmas in Arizona and take the week off.

On one of those days off as I was running errands, a friend I did Bible study with years prior, called and said, "Your name popped in my head while I was meditating this morning and wanted to give you a call."

I replied excitedly, saying, "I'm off this week, want to meet up for coffee?"

We arranged for a meeting the next day.

After a friendly hug, we hopped into a booth and grabbed some coffee and shared what happened in our lives that year. After my update, he shared. During his share, something very interesting happened. I became very present to a quiet call inside, completely unrelated to what he was talking about.

He stopped, and said, "You look confused."

I replied, "No, far from it. I just heard a quiet, still voice, a peace beyond all understanding ... and I need to sell my car ..."

He replied, "WHAT?!"

I continued. "And my home ... and trust. I can't believe it myself and I don't even have to think twice about it."

For context … on the way to the meeting, I was saying (out loud to myself) how much I loved driving my car. Yes, I talked to my car, out loud. HA! The car I bought was a white (i.e., a metaphorical) BLANK CANVAS before I really picked up painting.

It was another way my starving inner artist was attempting to express himself. I spent 2 hours per wheel creating custom center caps for the aftermarket wheels (non-Audi wheels) that I bought. I wanted the aftermarket wheels to look like they were supposed to be the wheels Audi should have put on from the factory. Finding the right wheels took me 6 months to find … that's a whole other story.

My starving inner artist was TRYING so hard to express himself.

Any artistic endeavor was a way of being able to fuel him.

My guess is, your starving inner artist is looking for any artistic endeavor as a way of getting fueled as well.

This book is a reminder to take on those creative endeavors that FUEL your soul.

I heard the inner call from inside and was heeding it and it provided me all the peace I needed for the decision.

Disclaimer 3: I'm not saying that after reading this book, you need to sell all your possessions and quit your job as THE ONLY WAY to feed your "starving inner artist." What I am inviting you to do is to express something through you with art that will help you see and hear things in the future that will often surprise you to live more of your best life.

Letting go

On the drive back, I said,"Wow, I am going to sell you," out loud to my car. I told you how much I LOVED that car and I DIDN'T even think twice about selling it.

When I got home, I said something similar: "I can't believe I'm going to sell you." Yes, out loud to my home. "And I KNOW it's what I need to do."

"It's ok to have things ... just don't let things have you" My car "HAD" me! My home "HAD" me.

Art cleared the way to "let go" of all the consumables I WAS DESPERATELY clinging to in my life in an attempt to feed the starving inner artist.

Funny story that came out during my travels of trust after the sale of my car and home.

Someone pointed out to me that when they asked me "why I loved my previous home," my FIRST response was "it's 10 minutes from the airport."

It was my most common response when anyone asked me about my home ...

I NEVER heard "that the thing I loved most about my home was that it got me as far away from it as possible" even though it was my most common response.

I couldn't wait to leave it! I was seeking freedom from it ...from the prison ... for years and I didn't even hear it.

Fascinating, right?!?!

As a result of accessing your inner artist, you will allow something new to express itself.

"Inner" Reflection Exercises

What are common responses that you make? Over the next week, ask friends to share common things they hear from you that you don't even hear yourself saying. Capture it here.

_____

_____

_____

What is something you have been looking towards outside that may be masking the inner calling?

_____

Go on, think about it ... I'll wait. :D

3. THE ARTIST'S PATH

And ... welcome back.

Going through these steps, you are going to begin expressing a part of yourself that hasn't been accessed in a while, ESPECIALLY if you don't consider yourself an artist.

Couple things to remember as you are embarking on this inward journey:

1.   Don't judge yourself

2.   Share your art with someone safe

3.   ENJOY the process

Remember: art is messy, life is messy ... if you mess up something, fix it and move on.

Now, as a reminder, I'm not saying you quit your day job to become an artist tomorrow because you are reading this book.

What I am saying is begin feeding that part of your soul that is LONGING to express itself.

It's why you have read up until now ... your inner artist really is listening. YEAH, YOU!

That is what you are being called to right now ... it's time you embrace that inner artist.

As we go into this artist section, another reminder and clarification is that when I talk about the starving inner artist, while I am referencing the painter throughout the book … you can apply it to any of the arts:

A musician,
A photographer,
A writer,
A singer,
A poet,
A potter,
A quilter,
A baker …

SO MANY other expressions of art. I use the example of painting throughout, though much of what you can do for other expressions can be done the same way.

1. Don't judge yourself

You might NOT know what art looks like for you because it has been so far pressed down and that is PERFECTLY fine.

Know that DEEP down you KNOW.

Your starving inner artist KNOWS.

Be gentle with yourself.

For those of you that have shoved it down inside without knowing how to access it … the remaining part of the book is for you.

Your Inner Artist Knows
You MAY KNOW CONSCIOUSLY exactly what art is looking to express itself through you, you have judged yourself that you aren't "good" at it so you leave it left unexpressed.

If that's you … start creating … or, if you occasionally create … increase the frequency.

I am going to offer strategies you can use to keep creating, SO ... the remaining part of the book is for you.

From my experience, I knew I LOVED art and yet I bought the "starving artist" narrative and THAT is what caused me to run from it for years.

Backstory
For me, I have ALWAYS loved art.

I would draw, color and get inspiration from anywhere and would create art anytime I could.

When I was a little child, my mom would take me to as many art classes that she could find.

Also, as an aside, my mom is an incredible artist. She's not a famous artist, only to me, she heeded the call and followed it and encouraged me to create art. I was able to get inspiration from some of the arts and crafts my mom would work on around the home.

Over the years, I would encourage her to sell the items she created and build a business around it, it was done that well. My entrepreneur was shining at an early age ... and I always loved business.

My mom did it for the love of creating ... there are no right or wrong answers on how you create art, ONLY THAT YOU CREATE art.

Find somewhere on the art spectrum for you ... start with doing it for the love first and listen to your inner artist to see where it might take you.

I always learned by doing and was curious to learn everywhere I looked.

Growing up, Dukes of Hazzard was a popular TV show. And, after visiting my parents' friends and playing with their kids Sean and Jennifer one evening, Sean showed me the paper General Lee he made. After he told me what he did, I came home and tried to do it myself. I experimented and even though it didn't turn out great, I discovered that I didn't enjoy creating paper car models as much as

I liked coloring or drawing.

As a child, I would regularly experiment with new types of art and it helped me see things differently and decide whether I wanted to continue or not. Art was something that allowed me to express myself in different ways and there was some art I enjoyed more than others. I loved art and doing art for the sake of doing art.

As I grew up, I put my "art" away, though it showed up in other ways like customizing my cars, in the aesthetics around my home.

How do your artistic expressions show up?

The long meandering path to expressing my art

After I enjoyed a record sales year in 2007, the next year would prove the most challenging of my sales career. The economic recession of 2008 hit my sales numbers and affected my sales confidence for the next 8 years. Today, I can now see how much of a gift that challenging year was.

Stories are powerful ... especially the stories you hear or tell yourself enough that end up affecting how you see yourself.

Until you can see the stories you are creating about your life, you can't change the stories if they aren't serving you.

IMPORTANT NOTE: THAT is why I am continuing throughout this book to encourage you to "Look at what's inside" so you can see it and, if it is no longer serving you, change it by intentionally focusing on improving it for what you DO want.

In 2008, I was bombarded with meeting after meeting with managers asking why I wasn't able to make my sales numbers amidst the great recession.

In those meetings, I kept hearing the stories they were telling me (as I heard them), which were:

"You're terrible at your job, why aren't you selling more?"

I was told those stories often enough that I started to believe them myself.

After enough of the stories, and on the verge of getting fired, I found another job. I was so scared of more meetings, of getting mentally beat up.

Now, in hindsight, I know the managers were trying to do their jobs, AND I have no hard feelings for them.

I forgave them.

Years ago, I heard the phrase "when you hold a grudge against someone, you are the one who holds onto the feelings."

I was forgiving them for me … so I could be free. I called many of them and actually talked to them and expressed that forgiveness in so many words or called and left a voicemail or simply let go of any ill feelings towards them.

When I "failed"
My identity was so tied up in succeeding over so much of my life, I didn't know what it was like to "fail."

I use "fail" in quotes because you never really fail, you (hopefully) learn about yourself and how you handle things in life.

That year was the toughest year I ever mentally faced.

FORTUNATELY, I was met with failure after failure that year.

I needed to figure out something else in my life, so I hired a coach.

In addition to advertising, psychology and personal development became an integral part of my life.

Coaching was selling to me … only instead of selling things to people through ads and consumption, I was helping clients find answers inside to questions they were asking. It was less about consumption and more about creation. Creating the life they wanted.

Going inward became my new passion

Whether I was being coached or coaching someone else, going inside to find answers became a passion for me.

Without realizing it, coaching was another form of art looking to be expressed.

Going inward to look at what's inside found its way into my art.

Discovering my starving "inner" artist

Years ago, I was teaching a "life balance workshop" and a woman named Nancy, who was attending, asked me about art, and I said I loved art. She asked if I painted and I said "no." She invited me to paint. I replied, "Ok, I will." It sounded like fun.

That was it; I said I would so I did.

I bought a canvas and some brushes and some paints.

When I let go and let it express itself organically without judging, I was able to simply paint for the sake of painting a canvas.

In the process, I saw the inner hurt and pain that I was pressing down and I saw what was inside. At least that is what I saw in my first painting.

After I was done, I EXCITEDLY texted Nancy and said, "I painted!"

She replied, "Show it to me."

I PROMPTLY froze after reading the text and every part of me didn't want ANYONE to see what I just painted. It was a representation of what I was feeling inside and didn't have words for. It felt SOOOOOO vulnerable to share because I saw something and wanted to not share it with anyone.

I eventually shared it. You can check the screenshot of the text here:

That first painting is called Emerging and you can find it on my site at

https://markjamnik.com/works/emerging

She was a safe person to share this with.

2. Share your art with someone safe OR an audience of ONE

When you are taking any of these artist exercises on for the first time, doing this in a safe space is essential. Whether that be with yourself or in a group.

Everyone must recognize the "set and setting" of the place so people can "look at what's inside" safely for them.

You can share on social media if you want; if you don't feel comfortable just yet and "feel naked," don't share it. I repeat, Don't Share it if you don't feel comfortable. I remember that feeling and sharing something so vulnerable can be "scary." Share when you are ready; start with someone safe.

I do a monthly event called "Paint with the Artist" (more about that in future chapters) where I teach the Subliminal Story Art process. I tell each person painting we are going to take a picture at the end and if you DON'T want to share, let your no, be NO! I HONOR them if they DON'T want to share it because they are listening to themselves.

The best person you can share it with is with an audience of one. Paint for you.

3. Enjoy the process

Do you remember when your inner artist expressed themselves?

For you it could have been singing, or dancing, or drawing, while for others it was riding bikes or running really fast.

That's what enjoying the process should be like, doing something that you fell in love with the very first time you did it. You might not have been great at it, yet something kept calling you back to do it.

You do it because you love doing it.

That is what I'm inviting you to do. If you enjoy the process, keep going. If you are forcing yourself to like the process because you think you should like the process, stop "shoulding" all over yourself and find a process you do like.

"Inner" Reflection Exercises

What is something simple you can practice?

_____

When will you commit to doing that? Add date here: __ / __ / __

4. WHAT IS SUBLIMINAL STORY ART

Subliminal Story Art is an abstract art sub-genre focused on emotion below the threshold of consciousness, tied together with storytelling. My mission with it is to make art more approachable, interactive and understandable.

Subliminal art, itself, exists within certain circles in the underground art scene, and may be described as genre-adjacent to mixed media painting.

Let's relate it to something we are all familiar with.

Paralleling the human condition
Underneath each person, is a story.

Art reflects life.

When you meet someone, that person is a compilation of life events that brought them in front of you.

They are SO MUCH more than their looks, their name, what they are wearing and a story that they may have just shared.

The more time you invest with them to get to know them, the more you discover about them and see who they are underneath all of the superficialities that we see.

There is a depth and richness inside each of us.

Underneath each person is a story.

Art reflects life.

The more you look at what's inside, you'll discover a depth and richness … and the more you see the beauty of the sameness of each of us … instead of our differences.

That depth and richness is a collection of a "mess" of emotions inside. We all have many emotions that we can all articulate through language. When you look life through the lens of emotions, you can see that we are all more the same than different.

As you connect with your inner artist, and look at what's inside, you can express those emotions in a way to express your "life masterpiece."

Underneath each painting, is a story.

Art reflects life.

Subliminal Story Art reflects life.

The idea behind Subliminal Story Art is to express more of the emotions and depth underneath the surface.

As you capture and share more of the depth of emotions underneath by writing them on a canvas, you create a work of art that expresses those emotions where others can connect to and relate (regardless of the similarities or differences their life story may have).

You'll be learning the 7 step process of the Subliminal Story Art process in the next chapter.

Before we go into the process, let's start with tying in the emotion.

Inspiration, Connection and Meaning
Subliminal Story Art is embedded with inspiration, connection and meaning in each work.

Here are some examples to consider for how I create art:

• Inspiration comes from life experiences.

- Connection comes from the amazing people I have an opportunity to meet each day.

- Meaning comes from the beauty of life and the depth that lies deep underneath.

When I start each work, I have no idea what the work will look like at the end.

Because I've done so much work in psychology and emotions, I feel like that's expressing itself through art and I'm actually able to give words to the feelings and emotions in my own way.

So start with the inspiration of the piece.

You can jot down notes of what words capture the emotion you want to express, and then architect the canvas for the words to add, then begin writing. Don't forget to snap a before photo of it and another one after, you get to painting.

Embed Inspiration
Inspiration can come from a variety of life experiences.

I am naturally drawn to simplicity, to nature and to the imperfection of life.

"Inner" Reflection Exercises

What are some of your own life experiences you can draw from?

Experience can include and is obviously not limited to:

- travel experiences domestically and/or internationally

- learning something new

- discovering something deeper within yourself (through books, coaching, or therapy)

- aligning with a cause

- sharing a passion of yours

- writing out goals and/or your vision

- capturing what makes you who you are

What inspires you in your life?

_____

_____

_____

Bringing the intangible into light

Every piece of art is completely subjective to the person, yet it actually gives something of a story now that people can connect to in a way that they might not have before.

Subliminal Story Art is helping to bring tangibility to what is typically intangible.

Art can be a platform to address difficult topics and bring light to the emotions inside the human experience.

When you bring light to something, you can actually transcend it as opposed to just letting it root itself in ourselves and saying, 'well, no one else is going to understand.

Painting helped me heal from perfectionism

In college, I struggled with OCD. I openly discuss my old battles, sharing the experience of taking 15 minutes to set, check, and reset my alarm clock every night while in the first year of college.

If I didn't do this routine, I feared I would oversleep and miss class.

I can speak about old struggles with OCD and perfectionism because I've lived through it and have transcended it. The reason I am so transparent about it is because I made it wrong and never wanted anyone to know for a long time. I used to think, "what's wrong with me?" If anyone knew … "what would they think?"

I'm no longer trying to hide or cover up this part about myself. I have embraced it and say, "Look, it's given me the opportunity to tie both sides of things together. I've got this totally OCD organized guy and I've also got this artist inside of me that's completely anything but organized." As a result of this, I have enjoyed being able to start difficult conversations concerning mental health through sharing my previous connection to OCD in college.

That challenge that I overcame in my life became the inspiration that turned into the work to reflect the main theme for the International Bi-Polar Disorder Foundation 2020 event: "Picasso Starry Night." While I didn't connect to being bipolar, I could relate to the cause with my severe case of OCD in college.

I captured the most important things to capture the essence of the foundation and portray in their art. Click the QR code or type the website link below and notice how I captured the dark AND light side of Mental Illness. In this case, the left side reflects the "darker" side of mental illness and transcends through the middle to the right side to reflect the "lighter" side and main focus for the foundation, where Empowerment, Advocacy, Education and Awareness are created through a caring community.

I want to make sure other people have the opportunity to speak out and know they are not alone. They can look at what's inside and share it with safe people to get the support they need. My work called Connection helped to raise funds for the organization as they look to support the over 450,000,000 people that suffer from mental illness.

https://markjamnik.com/works/connection

That's what art really is doing ... it's healing.

Art reflects life.

Embed Connection
Connection comes from the amazing people I have an opportunity to meet each day.

My abstract art pulls from the myriad of daily interactions, from the simplicity of a modern building with angles that depict modern man's version of perfection to the simplicity of how nature effortlessly blends death and life seamlessly to create the true definition of perfection ... imperfection.

This can also be a connection to yourself.

"Inner" Reflection Exercises

What are some of the things you LOVE doing?

1. _____

2. _____

3. _____

Seeing how much you love doing something written on canvas connects to a part of you that is looking to express itself.

If you love mountain biking or skiing, and you don't have to worry about your drawing skills, you can write the word "mountain bike." As you are painting, you'll know the words that bring you joy and as you paint that part of the work it will embed the joy of what's underneath.

Abstract art for me is healing.

It's free flowing … It's void of boundaries, boxes, the things that we know what it is.

All it needs to do is connect to something that means something to you.

Embed the meaning
Meaning comes from the beauty of life and the depth that lies deep underneath.

This colorful saturation of raw expressed meaning underneath the paint, is crucial to what forms the emotional connection to each work.

With an openness to what flows through my life and the continuous evolution of my art through active surrender to what may naturally arise, there's potential for ever-increasing categories and I look forward to the next spark of inspiration.

Here are a few Subliminal Story Art categories I created:

- Meaningful

- Causes

- Inspiration

- Retro

- Connection

- Experimental

- Brands

- Communities

- Cars

Meaningful

https://markjamnik.com/categories/meaningful-art/

Works reflect a deeper personal meaning for life experiences. Life comes down to the meaning that you give it. Some works are linked to multiple categories, though, as in life, things don't fit neatly into specific categories; something I was looking to do for a good portion of my life, make things fit into neat boxes that life is never intended to fit into.

Causes

https://markjamnik.com/categories/art-for-a-cause/

Works that connect to causes around my personal values. I have shared a certain dollar amount to the sale of the work to the International BiPolar Foundation. I also love giving $15 to Rock Bottom Hope for each new guest that attends my in-person Paint With The Artist series.

Inspiration

https://markjamnik.com/categories/inspirational-artwork-for-home/

Works that emotionally connect to what it means to be a human being. When I decided to sell my car and my home and trust … I painted 3 pieces that I set as an intention for my upcoming travels: Let Go (letting go of my car and home), Explore (which reflected the exploration of the traveling I was about to embark on) and Trust (which reflected the GREAT unknown I was going to step into).

Retro

https://markjamnik.com/categories/retro/

Works where I practiced painting before there were words, phrases underneath. These were my early experiences and while there is still a story of inspiration connected to them … I didn't start with the written words on canvas. It was painting to experience painting.

Connection

https://markjamnik.com/categories/connection/

Works that highlight how we connect to others and places. Connects with the local community and beyond.

Experimental

https://markjamnik.com/categories/experimental/

Works where I am attempting something new to learn and apply to future works.

Brands

https://markjamnik.com/categories/company-branded-art/

Works about companies that represent a deeper meaning from their team/staff/employees.

An incorporation of all coffee-shop logos, the visual and auditory stimuli floating through the air, and bubbling emotions, my artistic flow culminated in "Late for the Train". Named for the words veiled underneath, it now graces the coffee shop's gallery area.

Community

https://markjamnik.com/categories/art-and-community-engagement/

Works of places I have visited that have inspired me.

Auto Brands

https://markjamnik.com/categories/auto-branded-art/

Works inspired by cars where you can only see distinct images from popular car brands, by knowing where to look. To highlight my enthusiasm for cars, I developed Subliminal Story Art named "Four Rings," honoring Audi. It was inspired by my now sold 2013 Audi S4,

6-speed (pictured earlier in the book).

How Subliminal Story Art got its name

I wanted to call it Subliminal Story Art because I spent almost a decade and a half in the advertising world.

I spent 5 years in the coaching world as one of 100 global Tony Robbins coaches. Tony Robbins is a MASTER storyteller and I really started following influencers like Joe Polish and he shared many stories of how he got to be the Marketer that he became. People connect to stories.

"Subliminal" is often referenced inside of advertising; we often hear about the negative sides of subliminal ads — like flashing Coca-Cola on the screen so you crave it when you're in a movie theater. We've all heard the negative sides, so I wanted to create more of a positive side to it.

"Story" reflects the details of what created the details embedded in the painting.

"Art" is just that — the art I'm drawn to and created throughout my life.

Each painting depicts through bursts of color to inspire wonder, and be a reflection of what's underneath. It's great to say "here's what's actually underneath the painting in a way that actually inspires the painting and also has a story to tell."

It represents more closely the intention behind the art that is looking to express itself.

How Subliminal Story Art emerged

In 2012, after rigorous training, I was invited to serve as one of 100 active global Tony Robbins coaches. I specialized in coaching entrepreneurs, business owners and sales professionals that were looking to achieve their life's goals. We had a great group of coaches that were all looking to help and support each other grow and live their best lives.

During a coaching session of my own in 2013, my personal Tony Robbins coach encouraged me to start writing down the miracles I experienced — in a journal, on a sheet of paper, a tablet, anywhere — so I chose to use a canvas, and without knowing it, started the beginning of my work, which I later named, "Miracle Board."

After compiling the miracles on a canvas for over a year and a half, I just decided to paint over it one day. I said, "Oh, this would be neat if I just painted over it because then it's kind of locked and sealed in so there's a deeper meaning out of it" and as I started thinking more about that side of art, inside of art, art has a deeper meaning.

I stumbled upon what I now call Subliminal Story Art.

I remember one of the first strokes, I had no idea what I was going to paint. I just remember thinking "Oh my gosh, I'm breathing" when I took the first stroke because I don't know what it's going to do, what this is going to look like. I thought, "I know that wasn't a straight line and I have no idea where it's going, but I'm going to let whatever is supposed to come out, come out."

The vibrant colors produced in the end piece came from the build-up of miracles I recorded. If you look closely enough, some of the miracles shine through.

I have been asked what were some of the miracles I included … some were comments that people made to me, and others were those little coincidences that were amazing to be present with.

https://markjamnik.com/works/miracle-board/

Life in itself is a miracle and when you slow down to look for a miracle, you will find them everywhere.

Miracles are those little moments in life.

That random conversation you have with a stranger where you share something with them that they needed to hear or they mention a mutual acquaintance.

There was a song years ago that I always found touching by Sarah McLachlan called "Ordinary Miracles."

Listen to it to hear how simple life can be. I was moved to tears the last time I heard it because of how simple life really can be.

Audio break ...

Looking at the lens of life through the abundance of miracles can help you look kinder to those around you that may be less fortunate than you. Sometimes, that person you pass is simply looking to be seen. Saying "Hi" with a smile can potentially change their whole day. That is a miracle. The impact of a smile. Being kind to someone without knowing something about that person. Being kind to someone that is less than pleasant to you and realizing from a compassionate perspective that they may be having a hard day, week, month, year ...

There's so many little mini miracles in life and when you start looking for them, you see them everywhere.

How art is expressing through you
It's finding those little moments surrounding us everywhere and when we start looking for them, we slow down enough to actually recognize the present moment.

Many can get hypnotized into thinking the outer successes are the miracles. You know, those successes like having a thriving business or a career that is full of promotions or having that dream car or owning that beautiful home or being in an amazing relationship, or having a certain amount of money in the bank.

Those are great ... AND they are external.

Again, I'm not making any of the external things wrong, I'm simply sharing there is a richness to life of the miracles that come from inside.

There is something inside that is attempting to show itself through all of those external "successes."

When you "look at what's inside," you can see the beauty that exists within and turn that "messy" (emotion, situation, etc.) into your life masterpiece.

It's the art of life that is being expressed through the "paintbrush" of your presence.

You are being an artist of your life whether you are conscious of it or not. This process is helping you see the invisible that is going on underneath.

After painting the Miracle Board, a friend named Ryan who had similar aesthetics in his place, came over to visit and I showed him the painting and he said, "You did that?! I would buy that!"

I was shocked … I liked it and didn't expect that kind of reaction. I loved what showed up from the inside of me to express itself outside on a canvas.

As I reflect back on that moment, as I think on how I feel when I paint, letting go of time, I feel something this world can't touch.

That is why I wanted to share this process with others, so they feel something, something inside that is the need of any type of consumption on the outside.

"We are taught to be consumers … creators are who we are."

Life experiences, and healing are what I seek to share when I create works. I "let go and let God" express through me.

5. SUBLIMINAL STORY ART PROCESS

Subliminal Story Art starts with the end in mind. Encapsulate the deeper meaning of life inside the paintings. Create your own symbiotic relationship between the values of the heart and values of the head.

I use acrylic paint to begin hiding the written words' meaning, layer after layer. Sometimes the words, or pieces of words, peek through the abstract surface, and other times they stay hidden underneath, but all expressions form subliminal works.

You're going to learn the Subliminal Story Art 7 step process is broken into 3 categories: Painting, Sharing and Repeating.

Painting Process

1. Capture the emotion with words.

2. Start. Don't think. Feel.

3. Stop. After expression.

Sharing Process

4. Name it.

5. Write the story of what happened.

6. Share with safe people.

Repeating Process

7. Experiment.

Painting Process

Starting the canvas
You won't know what it's going to be because it's abstract. The words will help you encapsulate the emotion that the painting is going to express itself through.

Now that it doesn't have to look perfect and will simply express itself through you, let's walk through the process.

Step 1. Capture the emotion with words.
Each work starts out with words, phrases, verses, or a story ... and those words inform how the final artwork looks.

It is designed for you to "look at what's inside" and see "what's inside" on the canvas.

Now, I know that might seem really esoteric (or "Woo Woo").

Let's apply it right now for you.

"Inner" Reflection Exercises

What are you **excited** about?

• Is it a relationship?

• Is it a success in your company?

• Is it a trip you just got back from?

Those are just a few ideas; the list can go on and on.

_____

_____

_____

Now, imagine there is something you are **struggling** with or looking to depict.

Write down those words.

The words you write create the meaning and inspire the art.

This can be just as insightful if you are struggling or as if you are excited.

Here are some questions to consider to create your inspiration, connection and meaning:

What do you need to process?

_____

What do you want to celebrate?

_____

What do you want to share?

_____

Ok, write that down in your journal if you have one. If you don't have one, write it down on a sheet of paper.

The key is to capture the feelings.

Those are the first things that hit the blank canvas.

By seeing those words in your journal or on a sheet of paper, you can "look at what's inside."

Take a Before pic
Snap a picture of the before so you can see what's underneath.

Take an initial photo of each canvas before you start painting. This is an important part of the "before and after" project.

Set the mood
Once the subliminal layer is completed and photographed, create the type of mood through "music" or "silence" or talking with friends. I love listening to Sirius XM Radio and tune to Chill (channel 53) or Watercolors (channel 66) and let the music guide me. You can pick your favorite Spotify playlist or anything else you may enjoy.

There are times I'll just be immersed inside of the paint and other times where the music will inspire me and I'll just start dancing a little bit with the painting. I don't do it all the time, but if the music strikes me, I will.

That's how it starts … it's that easy.

Step 2. Start. Don't think. Feel.
Many (actually most) people spend most of their day thinking, analyzing, projecting. It's the thinking mind that wants whatever choice you make to be the right one.

Look, as a recovering perfectionist, I get how overanalyzing colors can affect what you do.

Abstract doesn't have a form, so don't overthink it.

Pick up a brush, pick up a color of paint, and start.

Painting gets you deeper into your heart.

Thinking about what to start with or where to start gets you in your head … the key here is to follow your heart and get OUT OF YOUR HEAD and into your heart to FEEL.

Let's start with two emotions on both ends of the "feeling" spectrum:

- Excitement
- Struggle

If you are sharing things you are **excited** about … pick out colors that express that. My guess is you are going to choose colors that are bright and when you see those brighter, happier colors, you'll feel excited.

If you are sharing things you are struggling with … pick out colors that express that. My guess is you are going to choose colors that are darker and less bright.

Here is an example of each … one that is EXCITABLE, one where I express the STRUGGLE.

Excited. Here is an example of Miracle Board and the vibrancy you read about in the last chapter: https://markjamnik.com/product/miracle-board

Struggle. In 2021, after selling my car and home and traveling, at times I was struggling with Comparison. Many things in my life were not like other things I was comparing myself to.

https://markjamnik.com/works/comparison-to-compassion

Art heals

After I created the Comparison to Compassion work, it really helped me to heal and share more of my story with others that might not know the whole story.

I have created other works that have helped me heal from attachment, from overwhelm, and from perfectionism.

Click on the QR code to find out this painting's story and how it helped me heal.

- Let Go
- Surrender
- Comparison to Compassion

Step 3. Stop. After expression.
When I begin, I start with the beginning and let the painting express the story underneath. I let go of creating a work that is perfect and simply paint.

Words, phrases, verses and stories that mean something to you show up in how you view life.

The more time you spend with each work, the more it comes to life and the more you can see things you haven't seen before.

Art imitates life.

There are times where I'll paint something and the colors or the texture don't quite do what I want it to do. When that is the case, I call it a treatment and later on paint over it.

Art imitates life.

When is it done?

A friend of mine asked, "How do you know when it's done?"

I said, "I just know."

The inner artist knows when it's done and when more work is needed.

There are 3 paths to Done:

- **Path 1: It's done.** - You finish it and LOVE it!

- **Path 2: It's not done, and needs more.** You take a break from painting, revisit it and repeat painting until you see "It's done."

- **Path 3: It's not done ... actually it IS done.** After I set it down and look at it the next day, I see it IS DONE.

Path 1: It's done.

There are times when I paint for 50 minutes and finish a work and say "it's done."

https://markjamnik.com/works/4-rings/

Path 2: It's not done, and needs more.

Other times, I painted, reached a stopping point and said, "That's good for now ... and it's not done." I will let it rest and pick it back up. I have added treatment (layer) and said, "Nope, still not it."

One of my favorite examples of this is my work called Gratitude.

After the first treatment, I didn't like how it looked, at all. It was a pale yellow with some green and red. The second treatment was very dull; grays and blues, yet HIGHLY textured. The third treatment got it to DONE and is now one of my top 3 paintings (and sellers for that matter). As I was painting, I knew this work was complete.

https://markjamnik.com/works/gratitude

Path 3: It's not done ... actually it IS done.

There are other times when you are painting and painting and you aren't sure WHAT you want it to look like, yet, it's not doing what you want it to do. So, when you get to a point where you are not sure where to go, stop and put it aside.

I decided to take a break after five hours to let it dry, convinced that the only answer was to paint over everything. After the paint solidified and dried, something told me to leave it — it was done.

When you step back from it, you MIGHT just find that ... it REALLY is done. That is exactly what happened with the work, Silk Road.

https://markjamnik.com/works/silk-road/

There is no definitive "this is when you stop and know that your Subliminal Story Art is complete."

The only definitive step is hearing the guidance from the inner artist and referencing the guide above to see what "state of done" your work is.

You will also find, the more you feed the starving inner artist, the less "starving" they will be.

Sharing Process

Step 4. Tell its story.
I began journaling in 2008 when I struggled with one of my toughest career years. I built up the practice of journaling and have applied the decade of practice into telling the story of each work so you can learn more about the inspiration, so you can connect to what I was experiencing and the meaning underneath. Even if it's just for you, writing and capturing the story will help you look at what's inside.

Step 5. Name it.
I create the name of the contribution canvases I take around Bend to

offer a prompt for the work. When I am creating my own work, there are times I'll pick a theme and then name it as I wrap up painting. I have also named it after I finished it and looked for a name, as in the case of the work, A Place Called Home.

https://markjamnik.com/works/a-place-called-home

Step 6. Share it.
Sharing your art is a powerful way to connect with someone else. If you aren't ready to share it with social media and if you need someone safe to share it with, email it to me at me@markjamnik. com. I remember the feeling when Nancy said, "Send it to me so I can see it," and the feeling I had of SO vulnerably sharing. I understand and am open to your sharing it with me personally or tagging #subliminalstoryart.

Keys to creating art:

- No time limits

- Capture emotion

- Music

- Don't judge yourself

- Create it for you

No time limits
Don't put a time limit on yourself. Time varies. Make sure you aren't up against any type of time window. When I paint, I like to give myself hours and hours of time. I don't always use all the time, I simply like to know it's there. When you are first starting, you might not need that much time, which is why many of my Paint with the Artist events (more on that in the next chapter) give guests enough time to work on and complete something in an hour and a half in most cases. I invite those that aren't finished to bring their paintings back the next month.

Capture Emotion
Decide on words that express more of the emotions you are feeling and need to look at. If you are struggling with something, write it down. If you are grateful for something, write it down ... AND, just like in life, you can have BOTH on the same canvas.

Music
Have your favorite music available to listen to to get inspired. Pick music that represents the mood of the painting. I love many different types of music; I really enjoy listening to Smooth Jazz or house music. When I paint, I prefer for my music to be void of words and simply like to move and paint with the rhythm of the music.

Don't judge yourself
Most people are HIGHLY critical of themselves. When I start off each Paint with the Artist class, there are one or two people that will say "they aren't good at it." I tell them to not judge themselves and that THEY SHOWED UP; that is a win! They are doing it. They aren't thinking about it.

Create it for you
You are creating art so that you can "look at what's inside." This isn't about creating something that someone else will say, "Wow, that's nice." I painted my original Miracle Board work for me. When I shared the story of my friend Ryan who came over and said, "YOU painted that?! I would buy that!" I never painted that work for Ryan. Ryan happened to like it. If someone HAPPENS to like it, GREAT! If not, if you LOVE it, that is you seeing the LOVE inside of you!

Reminder, I'm using painting as the example and you can apply this process for writing, or singing or other ... any other art.

Let go of expectations that other people will like it.

Create your art so you can "look at what's inside" and express it without the expectation that it will sell or be "liked" on Facebook or Instagram.

It's creation for the sake of creation and healing and/or sharing your own emotions for the sake of healing.

I enjoy painting and have more experience in sharing my painting stories and I wanted to keep it broad enough that you can apply it to your starving inner artist looking to express themselves.

Painting is a "fluid concept" (pun intended) and NOT a step by step. I wanted to offer some guideposts for you to get enough of the structure and then let you go to create.

Step 7 is for future inner artist works ... repeat steps 1-6.

Repeating Process

7. Experiment.
Each word. Each new inspiration. In the most basic, logistical sense, I invite you to try new things. I have spent hours placing written words using a Sharpie and then graduated to spending hours hand painting stencils to hand-pressed words on the canvas.

Find new tools
Try using things other than paint brushes. I used a paint stir stick for one painting and didn't use a paint brush.

https://markjamnik.com/works/routines

Stencils

The lettering resembles a typewritten, sophisticated effect for every word.

https://markjamnik.com/works/a-place-called-home

I Am Peace arose as a mindful mantra hybridizing with art; I hand-pressed each letter of the word "peace" into the shape of a peace sign. I also said, "I am Peace," as I laid the letters (not for everyone, it simply was a practice and a great reminder). It took hours to hand-press each letter.

https://markjamnik.com/works/i-am-peace

Scraper

Use different methods such as using a razor to alter the perceptual effects of acrylic on canvas.

Add Texture

You can eventually add in a mixed-media approach and expand to include matte and texture gels, sand, and others. I was going to use an old belt from a previous car; I thought it would be cool to see the ribs of the belt used somehow. I didn't end up using it as I was cleaning up my place years ago and wondered why I held onto an old belt. I share it simply to say you can add some cool texture using many different tools.

6. GETTING STARTED WITH SUBLIMINAL STORY ART

My mission as expressed is to make art more accessible, interactive and understandable.

Here are some ways you can get started with Subliminal Story Art.

Overview

Overview of things I'm sharing overall:
https://linktr.ee/subliminalstoryart

Inspiration

I live and breathe my work so you can follow along with this process and see stories of my life expressed on canvas.

The quickest way is to follow Inspiration on Mark Jamnik and follow my art and events on Subliminal Story Art.

https://www.instagram.com/markjamnik/

https://www.instagram.com/subliminalstoryart/

DIY Ideas

https://www.pinterest.com/markjamnik/

Connect on Pinterest where I showcase my art and share DIY strategies.

Paint with the Artist - DIY

Visit my site to get a painting supplies list of the supplies you'll need so you can do this for yourself or for a party. It includes the shopping list and the links to each product. Look forward to the inclusion of additional materials to naturally inspire yourself as you continue your artistic journey.

https://markjamnik.com/painting-supplies-list

Prints and Reprints
Throughout the book, I shared stories of the works. If you connected to the story or want to see others, you can view the work on my shop page and then after you find a work you like, you can read each painting's story.

Shop here: https://markjamnik.com/shop/

Legacy Commission^{SM}
If you have recently moved into a new home or want to reflect more of a legacy artwork, this is customized using the Subliminal Story Art process for you. This is Art inspired by you. Art designed to tell your family story. Art that emotionally touches you. Tell your family legacy through Subliminal Story Art. Create a legacy work for generations to come.

What a few clients have shared:

"It is not at all what I thought it would look like and it is EXACTLY what I wanted. The colors, the imagery, everything. I JUST LOVE IT!"
Heather M.

"It would be hard to top a gift so personal, heartfelt and meaningful." Jeff R.

What story would you want to subliminally share to truly make a work of art, a piece of your family legacy?

https://markjamnik.com/commission-works/

Local Artist Events (in Bend)

I live in Bend, OR, and I regularly share "Bend has a lot to offer, and I'm here to contribute." I love my community and found home.

If you are local to Bend, here are a number of ways to get started painting and interacting with Subliminal Story Art.

I share updates of where I host different events as well as post pictures from past events.

https://markjamnik.com/artist-events

Contribution Canvas^{SM}

I enjoy doing events like First Fridays and other markets where I talk with and invite people to participate in the event. Contribution Canvas events invite the participants at the events to contribute a word or a phrase to a canvas that will be eventually painted over.

This experience invites the community to contribute their thoughts around a centralized community theme. Contribution canvases are typically used at events like First Friday, special events like Bend Fashion Week or new Art Installations.

https://markjamnik.com/works-in-progress

I invite the community to contribute.

Even if you don't consider yourself a painter, look for events I host/participate within the local Bend community that I post on my Instagram where I bring a "Contribution Canvas" to events.

Paint With The Artist^{SM} **Series**

On the 2nd Thursday of every month, (as of this writing.)

People are creating their own Subliminal Story Art and the results are healing, they are transformative, they are therapeutic.

Sign up here: https://markjamnik.com/product/paint-with-the-artist

Here's what guests shared about the experience:

"I had a rough week and didn't know how much I needed a 'space' to work out what was going on in my head/heart. Thankful for the time spent with a good friend and the new friends we met along the way. Therapeutic in every way! I highly recommend this outlet to process your experiences in life!" Rachel

"The word I was given for the year 2022 was TRUST. I have been learning to trust my process while surrendering to God's will for my life. It is beautiful and sometimes messy ... Subliminal Story Art was an outlet for me to 'let go' and flow. My artwork seemed to change throughout the whole process but ultimately it became something beautiful that I loved ..." Erica

"Thoroughly enjoyed my time at Paint with the Artist event. Mark did a wonderful job connecting with people and inspiring them to let go as they created their pieces. I am looking forward to coming back." Kate

"My Paint with the Artist last week was a great experience! My painting really did look like what my experiences have felt like recently! Mark made sure we all felt comfortable and safe in order to paint from our inner experience. Thanks Mark!" Kerry

"I had a good time at aint with the artist, Mark really made me feel welcome and safe to express creative self!" Daniel

Read more reviews by scanning the QR above.

Collective Experience℠

The Collective experiences invite the organization to unify and share their collective thoughts around the company. Collective experiences are best used to align the collective goals and strategies of the organization. Capture the collective ideas around the company or cause. Foster a collective experience which invites your guests or team to express themselves through Subliminal Story Art. Discover the different community experiences created and let's brainstorm to see how we can develop your next company event or retreat to build community and connections. Visit what clients say about their Collective Experience by visiting the link below.

https://markjamnik.com/collective-experience

Fund Raising Events

This experience invites the organization to unify and share their collective thoughts around the company or cause. I organize events for non-profit organizations as fund raisers.

COTA members and volunteers were asked to share their #traillove and celebrate COTA's "30 Years of Trails" on a canvas. After the event, I read, review and create Subliminal Story Art from engaging with all of the participants. Fun Fact: I rode 30 minutes on my mountain bike with the canvas to paint it at the iconic "the Chicken" at Phil's Trailhead. I spent 3 hours in 40-degree temps engaging with the community as they rode by asking, "What are you doing?" Watch a fun video from the evening at the link below.

https://markjamnik.com/works/30-years-of-trails

7. YOUR MASTERPIECE

The "messiness on the inside" creates a "masterpiece on the outside."

Everything in your life … the challenges, the struggles … "all the things" got you to this moment.

Even if that moment isn't what you expected, it still got you to this point of the book, to hearing different ways to look at what's inside and follow the call from your starving inner artist.

When you picked up this book, you might not have seen yourself as an artist.

The goal of this book is to help you see yourself in YOUR own way, as an artist. A way to feed that starving "inner" artist.

My mission is to make art more accessible, interactive and understandable and I hope this book gives you resources to do that.

Your mission should you choose to accept it

Enter Mission Impossible theme music here.

Follow the call of your starving inner artist and turn the inside out through your art and express the beauty that lies within each of us.

After this book, take the details and start.

Discover your own liberation and continue to focus on growth, discovering new pieces of yourself as you create each work. This art is a pure manifestation of the rediscovery and reintegration of your whole Self; a synthesis of structure and flow, now embraced.

"Inner" Reflection Exercises

Will you accept the mission and feed the starving inner artist?

If yes, break it into bite size pieces.

If yes, here are a few next steps so you can follow through (ideally in the next 3-5 days).

What date will you get the supplies you need to begin? ___ /___

Do you need to research where to go? Yes / No

There are many different options to find art supply stores, from your local art supply store, to more of a national chain like Michael's, or Blick etc.

What date will you start painting (or creating)? ___ /___ /___

Great … add it to your calendar (on your phone or paper calendar).

Add the location.

When you schedule it, it becomes real. Think through what you will need so you have what you need to start.

Remember: You don't need to be a painter to be an artist.

You can do any type of art. All you need to do is reconnect to that art you loved as a child.

Take a moment now to write down 3-5 things you did as a child that you LOVED. Don't think too hard. Write down whatever comes to mind. If you need some ideas, read on.

Here is a random example before you start to get the wheels going.

When I was little, I remember someone in our neighborhood got a new appliance so there was a HUGE box to make whatever we wanted to make it into. We got creative and made that empty cardboard box into a world of possibilities.

I bought color books and loved to color.

I loved drawing monster trucks driving over cars.

Connect to that inner love for yourself and feed your inner artist.

Take a moment now to write down 3-5 things you did as a child that you LOVED:

1. _____

2. _____

3. _____

4. _____

5. _____

You don't need to do it perfectly. You simply need to start.

You don't need to share it on social media. You need to create for YOU. Look at what's inside.

A synthesis of structure and flow
Subliminal Story Art balances my love for organization and business acumen.

The struggles and the life journey have paved the path for another form of human connection: a linking of deep meaning combined with your inspiration. It's a practice that lies deep within the core of each human.

I love sharing my passion with others and I feel like we're all here to do and give our gift to the world.

"My art is my heart and my heart is guiding me."

I wanted to share my own stories as a way to inspire, connect and share the deeper meaning of why I wrote this book so that you can connect to that INNER ARTIST inside of you.

I often challenge others when they say they aren't artists ... I say, "You might not be a painter, though there is an inner artist that wants to express through what you do."

Find that expression and share it ...

Do everything with a level of LOVE and CARE and GRATITUDE and life will reflect those back to you.

Art is expressed through our lives.

I invite you to create your life as a masterpiece.

Here is the metaphorical brush, or whatever artistic tool you need to embrace your inner artist, and go paint a masterpiece through your life.

Create with love.

Mark and MY INNER ARTIST :D

ABOUT THE AUTHOR

Mark Jamnik grew up outside of Pittsburgh, PA and has loved art since he was a child. He loves blending structure with flow. He loves aesthetics. He loves traveling and his art has been inspired by 20 different countries — so far. He creates abstract art that pulls from the myriad of daily interactions, from the simplicity of a modern building with angles that depict modern man's version of perfection to the simplicity of how nature effortlessly blends death and life seamlessly to create the true definition of perfection ... imperfection. He takes and incorporates it all, to create Subliminal Story Art with deep meaning, similar to the beauty of life and the depth that lies deep underneath. Mark offers classes, creates original art, commissioned art embedded with their family legacy and creates collective experiences for companies to capture the deeper emotion of art. Mark lives and LOVES Bend, OR. He loves running year-round to keep his legs strong for all of his outdoor adventures. In summer time you can find him mountain biking, hiking and in winter, you will find him on the ski slopes.

www.ingramcontent.com/pod-product-compliance
Lightning Source LLC
Chambersburg PA
CBHW051645120626
46551CB00015B/2217